113TH CONGRESS *1st Session*	COMMITTEE PRINT	S. PRT. 113–22

WORKER SAFETY AND LABOR RIGHTS IN BANGLADESH'S GARMENT SECTOR

A MAJORITY STAFF REPORT

PREPARED FOR THE USE OF THE

COMMITTEE ON FOREIGN RELATIONS
UNITED STATES SENATE

ONE HUNDRED THIRTEENTH CONGRESS

FIRST SESSION

NOVEMBER 22, 2013

Printed for the use of the Committee on Foreign Relations

Available via World Wide Web:
http://www.gpoaccess.gov/congress/index.html

U.S. GOVERNMENT PRINTING OFFICE

WASHINGTON : 2013

85–633 PDF

For sale by the Superintendent of Documents, U.S. Government Printing Office
Internet: bookstore.gpo.gov   Phone: toll free (866) 512–1800; DC area (202) 512–1800
Fax: (202) 512–2104   Mail: Stop IDCC, Washington, DC 20402–0001

(II)

CONTENTS

LETTER OF TRANSMITTAL

UNITED STATES SENATE,
COMMITTEE ON FOREIGN RELATIONS,
Washington, DC, November 21, 2013.

DEAR COLLEAGUES: This report by the committee's majority staff examines the progress made on worker safety and labor rights in the Bangladesh garment industry since the Tazreen Fashions factory fire in November 2012 and the Rana Plaza factory collapse in April 2013. It is based on a field visit by the committee's majority staff to Bangladesh in August 2013, as well as extensive staff meetings with experts and stakeholders in Washington, D.C.

Bangladesh is a country of strategic interest to the United States. The continued growth of its garment sector is critical to supporting the country's economic development, a goal our country enthusiastically supports. While much attention has been paid to improving fire and building safety in the garment sector, more efforts are needed to improve labor rights and empower workers to ensure their own safety.

This report provides practical and timely recommendations for the U.S. Government and other stakeholders to safeguard and advance recent gains in labor rights for Bangladesh's garment workers.

Sincerely,

ROBERT MENENDEZ,
Chairman.

WORKER SAFETY AND LABOR RIGHTS IN BANGLADESH'S GARMENT SECTOR

EXECUTIVE SUMMARY

Two terrible tragedies occurring within 7 months of each other in the Bangladesh garment sector killed over 1,200 workers and galvanized the world's attention around the issue of worker safety in the country. Global retailers, foreign governments, and international organizations were spurred to action. These stakeholders launched several parallel initiatives to improve fire and building safety and efforts are underway to inspect every garment factory in Bangladesh. While much remains to be done to ensure that all of Bangladesh's factories are safe from fire or collapse, the mechanisms are in place, the political will exists, and vigilant observers are watching every step.

But ultimately, workers are best placed to oversee their own safety, and their empowerment to do so is best achieved through independent, representative labor unions. Unfortunately, union presence is still nominal and collective bargaining is virtually non-existent in Bangladesh's garment industry. A few small programs are working to change that, but far more will be required if Bangladesh's workers are to have truly safe, healthy, and decent working conditions. Principally, a fundamental shift in attitudes toward collective bargaining and the right to organize is required among all stakeholders, especially factory owners, global brands, and the government of Bangladesh.

Expanding the role of organized labor in Bangladesh now is imperative. An active labor movement is the best bulwark against another tragic accident. Improved awareness among American and European consumers is part of the push for better working conditions in Bangladesh. But the country's garment industry will increasingly produce for clients in markets that are not as discerning as European and American retailers when it comes to demanding compliance with health and safety standards, so strong unions will be needed to ensure the sustainability of current safety efforts. Most importantly, what happens in Bangladesh could have a dramatic ripple effect on the global apparel industry. Improving workers' rights in Bangladesh can help end the "race to the bottom" and lift labor standards in other growing economies like Burma and Vietnam.

KEY RECOMMENDATIONS

- The United States Government should hold the government of Bangladesh to the highest standards in implementing the action plan to reinstate U.S. Generalized System of Preferences (GSP) benefits, especially provisions pertaining to labor law reform and protecting the freedom of association and the rights to organize and bargain collectively.

- The United States government should increase funding for technical assistance programs in Bangladesh, such as those run by the AFL–CIO's Solidarity Center, that improve workers' capacity to organize and engage in collective bargaining.
- Apparel brands and retailers, especially those with very large operations in Bangladesh like Wal-Mart, Gap, and others in the Alliance for Bangladesh Worker Safety, should, in coordination with the ILO, launch long-term, well-resourced programs to educate their suppliers in Bangladesh on their expectation for compliance with laws allowing the right to organize unions and bargain collectively. They should also collectively develop and implement a policy of zero-tolerance for suppliers who consistently engage in anti-union activity.
    - The government of Bangladesh and the Bangladesh Garment Manufacturers and Exporters Association should immediately develop and implement tough and effective sanctions against factory owners who do not comply with Bangladeshi laws by engaging in anti-union activity, and advance progress in sanctioning owners who do not comply with required safety standards.
    - The next government of Bangladesh should act quickly to reform the existing legal framework, including labor laws for Export Processing Zones, to bring them into conformity with international labor standards.

Tazreen, Rana Plaza, and the Need for Organized Labor

On November 24, 2012, a fire started on the ground floor of the Tazreen Fashions factory in Bangladesh, where managers had illegally stored large mounds of fabric and yarn. Fire alarms went off on the factory's 8 floors, alerting the 1,150 workers inside of the mortal danger below. Yet managers on some floors, thinking it was a false alarm and worried about meeting production quotas, ordered workers to ignore the alarms and continue working. Workers who tried to escape down stairwells found them locked or choked with toxic smoke and impassable. Those workers could not demand safe working conditions from their employers because they had no voice, they had no union representation, and 112 lost their lives.[1]

Five months later and less than ten miles away, the workers of Rana Plaza refused to enter the building that housed their factories because they feared it would collapse. Managers threatened to withhold their pay and the workers, desperate for their meager average monthly income of $74 and lacking union representation and a unified voice, reluctantly entered the building. The building collapsed later that day, killing 1,131 and injuring hundreds. Simply put, had the workers of Tazreen Fashions or Rana Plaza belonged to strong, independent unions, they would not have perished in such tragic circumstances.

Since Rana Plaza, just 7 months ago, at least 27 garment workers have been killed and nearly 760 injured in factory fires across Bangladesh.

As a result of the Tazreen Fashions factory fire and the collapse of Rana Plaza, several important initiatives are now underway in Bangladesh to address fire and building safety in garment factories. But Bangladesh's garment workers will never have truly safe, healthy and decent working conditions until they have the ability to speak with a unified voice that is respected by their employers. Greater worker representation, in the form of labor unions, will give Bangladesh's garment workers the power to enforce their rights under the law. Unfortunately, many barriers still exist to greater worker representation in Bangladesh.

Chiefly, garment factory owners and managers have serious misperceptions regarding the role of organized labor and the potential of constructive labor relations. For their part, workers are largely uninformed about their rights to associate, organize, and bargain collectively. A sustained effort to educate employers and workers about these rights will be required before Bangladesh's garment factories can enjoy the benefits of an empowered workforce.

This report is based on a trip to Dhaka made by committee staff in late August 2013, where staff toured garment factories and met with workers, owners, Bangladeshi government officials, union organizers, labor activists, civil society groups, aid workers, brand representatives and U.S. diplomats. Committee staff also held many meetings in Washington, D.C. with retail bodies, labor groups and international organizations, among others. Senator Menendez also chaired a hearing on Bangladeshi labor issues on June 6, 2013. This report will briefly review the development and future potential of Bangladesh's ready-made garment (RMG) sector, evaluate current initiatives underway to improve fire and building safety in RMG factories, and assess efforts and barriers to enhancing workers' rights in the RMG industry.

THE PAST, PRESENT, AND FUTURE OF
BANGLADESH'S RMG INDUSTRY

Bangladesh's thriving RMG industry has grown from $12,000 in exports in 1978 to $21.5 billion in 2012-13, and now accounts for about 80 percent of total exports.[2] The Multifiber Arrangement (MFA), which started in 1974 and set quotas on garment exports to developed countries, spurred early growth in Bangladesh's RMG industry by providing competitive access to foreign markets. Bangladesh's low cost of labor and high capacity fueled growth when the quota system expired. The industry now directly employs some 4 million Bangladeshis, 80 percent of whom are women, mostly from poor rural households. The sector is estimated to support an additional 8 million tertiary jobs.[3]

With factories concentrated in and around the capital city of Dhaka, the RMG sector has been a major driver of urbanization in Bangladesh.[4] But such rapid growth created serious hazards: the demand for more capacity has led to garment factories sprouting up in apartment buildings and other multi-use structures not built to safely handle large numbers of workers and machines. While fire and building safety standards may have existed on the books, Bangladesh's government had neither the capacity nor the political will to enforce them.[5]

The major factor behind the lack of political will is the enormous political clout wielded by RMG factory owners in Bangladesh. According to one Bangladesh government official, nearly every Member of Parliament has close ties to factory owners and many are direct owners themselves. Many of Bangladesh's RMG factory owners are members of the elite, controlling significant media interests and exerting political influence.[6] Some are satisfied with the status quo, but others recognize the need for change: following the two recent tragedies, factory owners are reportedly now questioned by friends at social gatherings about their factory's level of safety compliance. Second- and third-generation factory owners are reportedly much more focused on compliance than first-generation entrepreneurs, but they only make up about 10-15 percent of owners.[7]

The garment sector is dominated by the Bangladesh Garment Manufacturers and Exporters Association (BGMEA), an industry group that was founded in 1983 and helped the government manage the administrative aspects of the quota system.[8] The BGMEA now enjoys tremendous regulatory powers and in some cases holds more sway over factory owners than the government: a factory owner recently refused orders by the Ministry of Labor to reinstate workers he had fired for union organizing and he rehired them only after the BGMEA threatened to revoke his ability to export.[9] As an association of factory owners, the BGMEA has historically opposed reforms that would give workers more rights. And while BGMEA leaders have said they are welcoming of unions in garment factories, they have yet to show a serious commitment respecting Bangladeshi laws as they relate to the right to bargain collectively and form unions.

The global outrage provoked by the tragedies of Tazreen and Rana Plaza did not appear to have any negative impact on the growth rate of Bangladesh's RMG exports, which saw a 24 percent year-on-year increase in the third quarter of 2013.[10] McKinsey & Company predicts that between the years 2010 and 2015 the sector will double, and then triple by 2020. While recognizing the advantages of its cheap labor and high capacity, the same McKinsey report also identifies several challenges facing the industry, including compliance problems with labor and environmental standards, poor transportation and energy infrastructure, and political instability and labor unrest due to oppressive work environments. Despite these issues, a large plurality of surveyed buyers identified Bangladesh as the future of RMG sourcing for their brands. In addition, a majority of buyers hope to expand into more sophisticated items like formal wear, requiring more skilled workers (there is currently a 25 percent shortage) and moving suppliers up the value chain, where there is less competition and higher profits.[11]

Continued growth of the RMG sector is critical for Bangladesh's development. Between the late 1970s and today, Bangladesh's poverty rate went from 70 percent to less than 40 percent and the average Bangladeshi went from living on $1 a day to more than $5 a day. It is no coincidence that the improvement of those numbers coincides with the rise of the RMG industry. RMG exports will continue to drive Bangladesh's GDP growth and provide jobs for rural poor, especially women, who are moving to the cities. Moving forward, the RMG sector promises to significantly boost economic development in Bangladesh and move it up the industrial value chain, just as it has for other economies around the globe, including Japan, South Korea and, more recently, China.

That is good news for the United States, for which Bangladesh is a country of strategic interest. Geographically, Bangladesh sits at the crossroads of South Asia and Southeast Asia, and it has extensive relations with both India and China. It has the world's seventh largest population and is the third-largest Muslim-majority nation. The United States shares many common strategic interests with Bangladesh, including global peace and security (Bangladesh is a top contributor of UN peacekeepers), counterterrorism, regional stability and global food security. Clearly, the sustained and responsible growth of Bangladesh's RMG sector is in the interests of the United States and the broader international community. But that growth is in danger if working conditions fail to improve. Consumers will reject clothing they believe is stained with the blood of Bangladeshi workers and global brands, anxious to protect their reputations, will be compelled to abandon the ''Made in Bangladesh'' label. This outcome can and must be avoided.

FIRE AND BUILDING SAFETY IN BANGLADESH'S RMG INDUSTRY

When the Tazreen Fashions factory burned down, it was the worst garment factory accident in Bangladesh's history. When Rana Plaza collapsed, it was the worst garment factory accident in world history. These tragedies spurred Bangladesh's government, global brands, the United States, other foreign governments, and international organizations into action. There are now several safety initiatives underway to ensure that none of the approximately 3,500 operating garment factories in Bangladesh will become another Tazreen or Rana Plaza. Nonetheless, the danger is still very real. A survey of factories released in June 2013 by the Bangladesh University of Engineering and Technology (BUET) found that 60 percent of factories were structurally vulnerable.[12] And again, abuses are widespread, as evident by the 27 garment workers who have died in factory fires since Rana Plaze collapsed.

BANGLADESH'S NATIONAL ACTION PLAN

The National Tripartite Plan of Action on Fire Safety and Structural Integrity (NAP), signed in July 2013 after Rana Plaza, updated a previous fire safety plan signed after Tazreen. The plan stipulates a series of commitments for the government of Bangladesh to meet by certain deadlines. For example, the government has upgraded its labor inspection department to a full directorate with a larger budget and is committed to create 800 positions, including 200 inspectors, by the end of 2013. However, by late November 2013 only four new labor inspectors had been hired since Tazreen, bringing the total to just 56.[13] The NAP also calls for inspection of all garment factories by the end of 2014, the creation of a factory information database, and establishment of a worker safety hotline. In addition, the BGMEA committed to creating a ''transparent and accountable'' system for sub-contracting in the industry.[14]

Unauthorized sub-contracting is a significant challenge in Bangladesh's RMG industry. Factory owners will often take more orders than they have capacity for and send the excess work to subcontractors. This may not be a problem when those subcontractors are known to the brand and have been properly inspected for labor and safety compliance. But owners may also subcontract to unknown factories that operate in the shadows of Bangladesh's RMG industry. These factories are often the most dangerous in terms of worker safety and the most egregious violators of worker rights. Despite the efforts of the brands to make clear to suppliers that they do not tolerate unauthorized sub-contracting, the practice continues. The situation provides a strong incentive for brands to facilitate the formation and expansion of independent factory-level unions, which would serve as a bulwark against unauthorized subcontracting.

In the longer term, the government of Bangladesh also plans to develop a new 535-acre industrial zone for the RMG sector. The zone will feature all-new, up-to-code buildings where factory owners currently operating in vulnerable buildings will supposedly relocate. However, factory locations in the park will be highly coveted and, according to one Bangladeshi government official, may end up going to owners with political connections and money—a very different group from owners that cannot afford to fix their current factories and operate outside the margins of Bangladeshi law.[15]

U.S., EU, ILO PLANS

Citing Bangladesh's failure to improve worker safety and labor rights, in June 2013 the United States government (USG) suspended Bangladesh's eligibility for tariff benefits under the Generalized System of Preferences (GSP) program.[16] Since garments do not receive tariff benefits under the GSP program, suspension of GSP did not impact Bangladesh's over $4 billion worth of annual RMG exports to the United States, however it did effect about $40 million worth of imports in ceramics, tobacco, and other products. But garments receive benefits under the EU's GSP program, and suspension of U.S. GSP raised fears in Bangladesh that the EU might follow suit. In July 2013 the USG released its Bangladesh Action Plan 2013, which sets out several safety and labor benchmarks for Bangladesh to achieve before GSP benefits could be reinstated. Many of the benchmarks match those in the NAP, such as vastly increasing the number of inspectors, inspecting all factories, creating an inspection database, and establishing an effective mechanism for worker safety complaints.[17] As of this report's publication, none of those GSP action plan benchmarks had been met. The GSP action plan also includes several measures on labor rights, discussed below.

The ILO, along with the EU and the United States, supported development of another worker safety and rights agreement called the Sustainability Compact, which was signed by the government of Bangladesh in July 2013. It shares many aspects of the NAP and the GSP action plan, and an official review of Bangladesh's progress will occur sometime in 2014.[18] Progress on implementation of the NAP, GSP action plan, and Sustainability Compact is closely monitored by the international community. Every few weeks a "3+5" assessment meeting takes place, attended by Bangladesh's Secretaries of Commerce, Labor, and Foreign Affairs on one side and Ambassadors from the United States, EU, Netherlands, United Kingdom and Canada on the other. The diplomats engage with the Secretaries on next steps and flag deficiencies or problems in implementation of the plans.[19]

To help Bangladesh with inspections and safety improvements in factories, in October 2013 the International Labor Organization (ILO) launched a $24 million, three-and-a-half year initiative called "Improving Working Conditions in the Ready-Made Garment Sector" (RMGP). The program will assist with inspections of approximately half of Bangladesh's garment factories by helping to stand up 30 structural assessment teams. The program will also work to improve the government's inspection mechanisms, build occupational health and safety awareness in factories, and provide compensation and skills training for victims of the Tazreen and Rana Plaza accidents.[20] The compensation mechanism will establish an international trust fund into which retailers, governments, and others can donate. Some 3,900 claimants have already had their biodata collected and bank accounts established in their names, and full compensation of victims will require approximately $40 million from donors.[21]

APPAREL COMPANIES AND WORKER SAFETY

Apparel brands launched two major worker safety initiatives after Rana Plaza. Over 100 companies, mostly European but joined by a few American firms such as PVH (parent company of Calvin Klein, Tommy Hilfiger and Izod), American Eagle, and Abercrombie & Fitch, signed on to an initiative called the Accord on Fire and Building Safety in Bangladesh ("the Accord"). Over 20 American retailers, including Wal-Mart, Gap, Target and JC Penny, declined to join the Accord but formed a similar initiative called the Alliance for Bangladesh Worker Safety ("the Alliance"). Together, the apparel brands and retailers in the Accord and the Alliance source from approximately half of the active garment factories in Bangladesh. The firms in the Accord source from about 1,500 factories and the Alliance's members source from nearly 700 factories; the two share about 350 factories.[22]

Both programs are developing inspection standards for fire and building safety in supplier factories, and have harmonized their standards with each other and the government of Bangladesh.[23] Both programs will last 5 years, require membership fees, perform full inspections of all factories, provide safety training for all workers and managers, and have mechanisms, such as low-cost loans, for remediation of non-compliant factories.[24] Each of these initiatives will spend millions of dollars pursuing improved safety objectives in their supplier factories. Some observers are concerned that factory owners may refuse remediation mandated by Alliance or Accord members and source to a less scrupulous buyer. It will be critical for the government of Bangladesh and BGMEA to impose effective sanctions in these situations.

One key difference between the Accord and the Alliance is the assignment of decision-making authority. The Accord centralizes its decision-making authority in its executive while the Alliance leaves most decisions up to individual retailers. For example, the Accord's executive board is responsible for hiring inspectors and deciding whether Accord members can continue sourcing from a factory based on inspection results (in at least one case so far, the Accord's members have ceased doing business with a factory that refused to address deficiencies found during inspection).[25] The Accord also gives an oversight role to trade union signatories, who can initiate binding arbitration against another member of the Accord for non-compliance with the terms of the agreement.[26]

In the Alliance, individual members are responsible for hiring Alliance-approved inspectors. Alliance members can choose whether or not to continue doing business with a factory based on inspection results, and only retailers can initiate arbitration against other retailers, which at worst results in expulsion from the Alliance.

While it is too early to tell whether the different approaches being pursued by the Accord and the Alliance will result in different outcomes regarding improvements in fire and building safety at their supplier factories in Bangladesh, other differences in governance structure and worker empowerment are substantial.

LABOR RIGHTS AND RELATIONS IN BANGLADESH'S RMG INDUSTRY

Bangladesh has a troubled history of labor relations. In the 1970s, the jute industry played a similar role as the RMG industry does today, accounting for nearly 90 percent of all exports and driving GDP growth.[27] While a combination of factors contributed to the jute industry's decline, RMG factory owners and BGMEA officials will commonly cite a single reason: labor unions. Decades ago, labor unions in jute factories were highly politicized and controlled or influenced by political forces; plant-level unions competed fiercely and would bring production to a halt for reasons unrelated to working conditions or labor rights.[28]

RMG factory owners and some government officials fear that the past will repeat itself in the RMG industry. Some owners in Dhaka claim workers do not need unions because working conditions are so good.[29] Others owners fear they will lose control of their factories if workers unionize. The bottom line is that freedom of association and collective bargaining are not well understood and unions are generally maligned.

There is cause for hope. The RMG industry has made progress in the past on moving to eliminate the use of child labor, allowing workers to take bathroom breaks, and keeping gates unlocked.[30] But workers' rights to associate, organize, and engage in collective bargaining have been largely ignored for the last 25 years, and the current state of misunderstanding and mistrust about the proper roles and responsibilities of unions will require tremendous and sustained efforts to overcome. While some small steps have been taken, much remains to be done.

LABOR LAW REFORM

On July 15, 2013, Bangladesh's Parliament passed reforms to the country's labor law, and the government is now writing the implementing regulations. While the reforms changed 87 sections of existing law—a number often cited by Bangladeshi officials—it fell short of expectations, and most observers agree that Bangladesh did just enough to allow the ILO to approve a Better Work program (discussed below). The ILO's initial review of the legislation found that, among other things, the new labor law eliminates the requirement for the government to send factory owners the names of union leaders registering unions in their factories, allows union leaders to call on outside experts for advice during collective bargaining, and improves several provisions on workplace safety and health. Overall, the ILO found that ''the amendments did address some of the ILO's specific concerns, while falling short of several important steps called for by the ILO.'' [31]

In its review, the AFL-CIO criticized the reform package for several reasons: it does not make the union registration process any easier (though the government has nominally increased approvals of applications); it does not allow union representatives fired from their jobs to keep their factory-level union membership while they contest their termination; trade unions are required to receive government permission to affiliate with an international union or receive financial assistance from foreign groups; and provisions relating to severance payments were actually made more restrictive than existing law. [32]

The GSP action plan also includes a provision requiring the government of Bangladesh to bring the labor law in Export Processing Zones (EPZs) into conformity with international standards and, until that time, issue regulations to protect freedom of association in the EPZs. [33] The EPZs are special industrial zones that were set up to attract foreign investors in the early days of Bangladesh's RMG industry. Workers inside the zones enjoy safer working conditions and slightly better pay than those outside, but at the cost of their fundamental labor rights. [34] The USG's position is that there is no need to continue to limit workers' rights in the EPZs, and Bangladesh should remove these restrictions immediately.

Bangladesh still has a long way to go in reforming its labor laws to meet international standards. The recently passed amendments should not be considered sufficient as they do not meet the labor law reform requirement in the GSP action plan. Furthermore, this committee, the United States government and the international community will be watching closely as Bangladesh writes the implementing regulations for the labor reforms. The committee welcomes ILO assistance for Bangladesh in this effort.

The GSP action plan and the Sustainability Compact also have several measures on labor rights in the RMG sector. Benchmarks include: reforming the labor law to address concerns related to freedom of association and collective bargaining; expeditiously and transparently registering new unions and protecting workers from anti-union activity; reporting anti-union activity on a public database; implementing mechanisms to prevent harassment of labor activists and leaders; and advancing the investigation into the murder of labor activist Aminul Islam. [35]

As of this report's publication, the government of Bangladesh had made little progress on any of those benchmarks, save for nominally increasing union registrations. However, Bangladesh did make progress on some benchmarks, such as registering non-gov-

ernmental labor organizations that meet administrative require-
ments and dropping criminal charges against labor activists. If the
U.S. Congress renews the GSP program, which has expired, the
U.S. Trade Representative is expected to conduct an official review
of Bangladesh's progress on the GSP action plan and announce a
determination on its eligibility in mid-2014.[36]

UNION REGISTRATION AND ORGANIZATION

To its credit, the government of Bangladesh has made some
progress in registering new unions. Whereas only two new unions
were registered between 2011 and 2012, 59 new unions were registered between January and October 2013, with 30 applications
pending.[37] The United States—through the AFL–CIO's Solidarity
Center—and other international donors, in conjunction with the
ILO, should take advantage of this opening by increasing labor-related technical assistance that builds organizing capacity. Factory-
level union organizers have expressed an urgent need for more
training on organizing, collective bargaining negotiations, and labor
law.[38]

Though the registration of unions is a welcome development, the
USG and other international observers must continue to pressure
the government of Bangladesh on its commitment. Specifically, at
least five of the newly registered unions are management-spon-
sored and meant to compete with and crowd out independent, representative unions. In one case, the management tried to apply for
the factory's full quota of three unions, which would have left no
space for a genuine union.[39]

National union federations in Bangladesh are moving quickly to
expand and organize new factory-level unions. Previously, they cul-
tivated union leaders by identifying workers respected by their
peers, began training them, and tested them with increasing responsibilities while assessing their leadership abilities. But now
factory workers are increasingly self-selecting leaders, who approach the federations for assistance with organizing and capacity
building. And whereas before union organizers had to go door-to-
door in workers' neighborhoods to organize, in many cases the
workers now proactively seek out the union representatives.[40]

But barriers still exist, and many employers are actively sup-
pressing unions in their factories. There have been several docu-
mented cases of anti-union activity in different factories and untold
numbers of undocumented cases. Anti-union tactics range from
harassment and termination of unionized workers to the beating of
union leaders. In one case, a female union leader was taken to a
hospital bleeding and semi-conscious after thugs attacked her with
a pair of cutting shears. Other factory-level union leaders, many
just in their 20s, say that they would never have tried to organize
a union had they known managers would make life so difficult for
them. Some have been intimidated by goons, harassed by managers, isolated from other workers and threatened with termination. But other organizers have success stories: management has
ended physical punishments, stopped cursing at employees, and
dispensed holiday bonuses for the first time.[41]

APPAREL COMPANIES AND LABOR RIGHTS

The Alliance and Accord plans, while sharing similarities in their approach to fire and building safety inspection, have a few important differences when it comes to worker participation and empowerment. For example, while the Accord's executive committee has equal representation between trade union signatories and corporate signatories (three seats each), the Alliance's executive committee has no representation by worker rights organizations. Furthermore, the Accord's safety training teams include union representatives that educate workers about their right to refuse work in a dangerous building, which could lead to broader discussions on worker's rights. At present, the Alliance's training teams do not include union representatives; neither initiative explicitly includes training on freedom of association, collective bargaining, and the role of unions.

The Alliance plans to engage with workers principally through Worker Participation Committees (WPCs). WPCs are platforms for worker-management dialogue and are required by Bangladeshi law. Workers elect their representatives to the WPC, which then meets with management once every month or two to discuss worker concerns. While WPCs give workers some voice, they are essentially powerless and have no leverage when dealing with management. There are also instances of management influencing the selection of worker representatives to WPCs. WPCs are clearly no substitute for genuine representation of workers' interests through unions and collective bargaining agreements.

Both the Accord and the Alliance should include education on freedom of association, organization, and collective bargaining in their training curriculum and ensure that the workers in their factories are aware of their rights and the differences between WPCs and genuine unions. They should also educate owners and managers on how to maintain constructive and cooperative relations with independent labor unions in their factories. Improved worker-management dialogue will be critical to ensuring safe, healthy, and decent working conditions in Bangladesh's expanding RMG sector.

LABOR-RELATED FOREIGN ASSISTANCE

While funding for labor-related technical assistance programming in Bangladesh's RMG sector has increased recently, the overall sums remain small. The USG's main implementing partner for RMG labor-related programming in Bangladesh is the AFL–CIO's Solidarity Center. The Solidary Center is currently implementing two multi-year programs, with a combined $4 million, which seek to strengthen workers' rights of freedom of association by enabling union organization and collective bargaining. These objectives are being pursued by the Solidarity Center primarily through training, capacity building, and legal assistance.[42] As of November 2013 these programs had trained over 50 full-time organizers and held dozens of organizational capacity trainings for new unions.[43] The program has financially supported 20 organizers and hopes to support 65 more. Training of organizers was previously constrained by the inability to register new factory-level unions. Now that the government of Bangladesh is allowing unions to register, the Solidarity Center expects to scale up its operations and train more organizers, with the goal of registering 500 new unions over the next 5 years.

In addition, in June 2013 the Department of Labor announced a $2.5 million program to strengthen enforcement of fire of building safety standards by building the capacity of worker organizations to monitor safety violations. The funding will be split between grants to the Solidarity Center ($1 million) and the ILO ($1.5 million).[44]

Few other countries and international organizations have programs promoting workers' rights in Bangladesh. The Dutch trade union Federatie Nederlandse Vakbeweging (FNV) has a four-year program to support training of Bangladeshi partner unions. The Clean Clothes Campaign, which is part of the Accord, also has a four-year program to support worker organization in Bangladesh's RMG industry.[45] Clearly, there is a need for more foreign governments and international organizations to finance and implement programs supporting freedom of association and collective bargaining.

As a result of the passage of the labor law reforms and the registration of new unions, the ILO, in partnership with the International Finance Corporation (IFC), launched a Better Work Bangladesh program in October 2013. The Better Work program will focus on industrial relations and worker concerns like hours and wages.[46] The program will work with participating retail brands to select factories, clustered in a few geographic areas, which are deemed qualified for the program after undergoing inspections. Many retailers are anxious for their factories to participate in the program, and some may even compel their suppliers to join. The committee encourages American brands and retailers, especially members of the Alliance, to urge their suppliers to join Better Work.

After selection, Better Work teams will enter the factories and provide advisory services and training to management and workers while ensuring compliance with labor standards and facilitating strong social dialogue. For example, Better Work teams will help factories implement the new labor law by educating workers on how WPCs function and the difference between WPCs and labor unions.[47] As WPCs have been used to crowd out unions in the past, this will be an important distinction for workers to learn.

Better Work teams will begin inspecting factories in the second quarter of 2014. The program plans to scale up to 500 factories by its third year. The ILO has created a "Framework for Continuous Improvement" that has targets Bangladesh must meet in order for the Better Work program to continue. The commitments associated with the framework are derived from the NAP, the GSP action plan, and the Sustainability Compact.[48] The establishment of a Better Work program in Bangladesh is a positive development that promises to pay serious dividends in improving working conditions in RMG factories, especially where there are active unions in place.

CONCLUSION

The various worker safety programs initiated in the wake of Tazreen and Rana Plaza have the potential to considerably improve the safety of Bangladesh's garment factories in the short term. But these gains may be lost without strong worker oversight in the form of independent unions.

Some progress has been made recently by Bangladesh's fledgling unions, but much more remains to be done. The biggest obstacles to the future development of unions are the current anti-union mindset of factory owners and a fear and lack of awareness among factory workers. These barriers will take some time to overcome. Progress is clearly possible, though, with sustained and genuine efforts by the governments of the United States, Bangladesh, and other countries, as well as apparel brands and retailers.

International pressure is growing against the government of Bangladesh, apparel brands and factory owners in Bangladesh. Bangladesh's garment sector may not be able to withstand another tragedy on the scale of Tazreen and Rana Plaza. The surest way to guarantee the success of the apparel industry is to avoid another disaster by promoting and protecting labor rights now, while the world's attention is on Bangladesh. The present opportunity to improve working conditions in Bangladesh cannot be squandered.

FULL LIST OF RECOMMENDATIONS

For the United States Government

- The USG should hold the government of Bangladesh to the highest standards in implementing the GSP action plan, especially provisions pertaining to labor law reform and protecting the freedom of association and the rights to organize and bargain collectively.
- The USG should increase funding for technical assistance programs in Bangladesh, such as those run by the AFL-CIO's Solidarity Center, that improve workers' capacity to organize and engage in collective bargaining.
- The U.S. Department of State should place a full-time labor attaché from the U.S. Department of Labor at its mission in Dhaka.

For Apparel Brands and Retailers

- Apparel brands and retailers should aggressively continue implementing inspection and remediation programs focused on fire and building safety in their suppliers factories in Bangladesh.
- Apparel brands and retailers, especially those with very large operations in Bangladesh like Wal-Mart, Gap, and others in the Alliance for Bangladesh Worker Safety, should, in coordination with the ILO, launch long-term, well-resourced programs to educate their suppliers of their expectation for compliance with laws allowing the right to organize unions and bargain collectively.
- Apparel brands and retailers, in coordination with the ILO and representative unions, should launch a program to educate garment factory workers about their rights and responsibilities with respect to freedom of association, organization, and collective bargaining.

- Apparel brands and retailers should also collectively develop and implement a policy of zero-tolerance for suppliers who consistently engage in anti-union activity.

For the Government of Bangladesh and BGMEA

- The government of Bangladesh and the BGMEA should immediately develop and implement tough and effective sanctions against factory owners who engage in anti-union activity, and advance progress in sanctioning owners who do not comply with required safety standards.
- The government of Bangladesh and the BGMEA, in coordination with the ILO, should undertake a program to educate garment factory owners on the constructive role of labor unions in garment factories and endeavor to ensure that anti-union activity is eradicated.
- The government of Bangladesh and the BGMEA, in coordination with the ILO and representative unions, should sponsor a program to educate garment factory workers about their rights and responsibilities with respect to freedom of association, organization, and collective bargaining.
- The next government of Bangladesh should act quickly to reform existing labor laws, including EPZ labor laws, to bring them into conformity with international labor standards.

NOTES

[1] Julfikar Ali Manik and Jim Yardley, "Bangladesh Finds Gross Negligence in Factory Fire," New York Times, December 17, 2012, accessed November 20, 2013, http://www.nytimes.com/2012/12/18/world/asia/bangladesh-factory-fire-caused-by-gross-negligence.html

[2] "RMG: The Mainstay of Bangladesh Economy." Bangladesh Garment Manufacturers and Exporters Association, accessed November 20, 2013, http://www.bgmea.com.bd/home/pages/Strengths#.Uoz348ReZLA

[3] SFRC staff discussion, Dhaka, August 2013.

[4] AMRF Society, "Workers' Voice Report 2013: Insight into Life and Livelihood of Bangladesh's RMG Workers." Paper presented to SFRC staff, September 25, 2013.

[5] SFRC staff discussion, Dhaka, August 2013.

[6] Yardley, Jim. "Garment Trade Wields Power in Bangladesh." New York Times, July 24, 2013, accessed November 21, 2013, http://www.nytimes.com/2013/07/25/world/asia/garment-trade-wields-power-in-bangladesh.html

[7] SFRC staff discussion, Dhaka, August 2013.

[8] Yardley, Jim. "Garment Trade Wields Power in Bangladesh." New York Times, July 24, 2013, accessed November 21, 2013, http://www.nytimes.com/2013/07/25/world/asia/garment-trade-wields-power-in-bangladesh.html

[9] SFRC staff discussion, Dhaka, August 2013.

[10] Al-Mahmood, Syed Zain. "Bangladesh Exports Undeterred." The Wall Street Journal, October 10, 2013, accessed November 21, 2013, http://online.wsj.com/news/articles/SB30001424052702304500404579127314213623956 http://online.wsj.com/news/articles/SB30001424052702304500404579127314213623956

[11] Achim Berg, Saskia Hedrich, and Thomas Tochtermann, "Bangladesh: The next hot spot in apparel sourcing?," Mckinsey & Company, March 2012, accessed November 21, 2012,

[12] Burke, Jason. "Majority of Bangladesh garment factories 'vulnerable to collapse." The Guardian, June 03, 2015, accessed November 21, 2013, http://www.theguardian.com/world/2013/jun/03/bangladesh-garment-factories-vulnerable-collapse

[13] SFRC staff discussion, Washington, D.C. November 2013.

[14] "National Tripartite Plan of Action on Fire Safety and Structural Integrity in the Ready-Made Garment Sector in Bangladesh." Accessed November 21, 2013, http://www.ilo.org/wcmsp5/groups/public/_asia/_ro-bangkok/_ilo-dhaka/documents/genericdocument/wcms—221543.pdf

[15] SFRC staff discussion, Dhaka, August 2013.

[16] Froman, Michael. U.S. Trade Representative , "ustr.gov." June 2013, accessed November 21, 2013, http://www.ustr.gov/about-us/press-office/press-releases/2013/june/michael-froman-gsp-bangladesh.

[17] Della, Gloria. U.S. Department of Labor News Release, "ILAB," July 29, 2013, accessed November 21, 2013, http://www.dol.gov/opa/media/press/ilab/ILAB20131494.htm.

16

[18] European Union Joint Statement, "Staying engaged: A Sustainability Compact for continuous improvements in labour rights and factory safety in the Ready-Made Garment and Knitwear Industry in Bangladesh." Accessed November 21, 2013.
http://trade.ec.europa.eu/doclib/docs/2013/july/tradoc—151601.pdf

[19] Staff discussion in Washington, D.C. November 2013

[20] International Labor Organization. "Towards a safer garment industry in Bangladesh." October 22, 2013, 2013.
http://www.ilo.org/global/about-the-ilo/activities/all/safer-garment-industry-in-bangladesh/lang--en/index.htm

[21] Staff discussion in Washington, D.C. November 2013

[22] Staff discussion in Washington, D.C. November 2013

[23] Al-Mahmood, Syed Zain. "Safety Groups Agree on Common Standards for Bangladesh Garment Factories," Wall Street Journal, November 20, 2013, accessed November 21, 2012
http://online.wsj.com/news/articles/SB10001424052702304337404579209954273740442

[24] "Accord on Fire and Building Safety in Bangladesh."
http://www.bangladeshaccord.org/; "Members Agreement of Alliance on Bangladesh Worker Safety."
http://www.bangladeshworkersafety.org

[25] Accord on Fire and Building Safety in Bangladesh. Press release. October 14, 2013.
http://www.bangladeshaccord.org

[26] "Accord on Fire and Building Safety in Bangladesh."
http://www.bangladeshaccord.org

[27] SFRC staff discussion, Dhaka, August 2013.

[28] SFRC staff discussion, Dhaka, August 2013.

[29] SFRC staff discussion, Dhaka, August 2013.

[30] SFRC staff discussion, Dhaka, August 2013.

[31] International Labor Organization. "ILO statement on reform of Bangladesh labour law." July 22, 2013, 2013.
http://www.ilo.org/global/about-the-ilo/media-centre/statements-and-speeches/WCMS—218067/lang--en/index.htm

[32] Drake, Celeste. "The AFL-CIO Reacts to Recently Passed Amendments to the Bangladesh Labor Law of 2006." AFL-CIO NOW July 23, 2013, 2013, accessed 21 Nov 2013, The-AFL-CIO-Reacts-to-Recently-Passed-Amendments-to-the-Bangladesh-Labor-Law-of-2006

[33] Della, Gloria. U.S. Department of Labor [News Release], "ILAB," July 29, 2013, accessed November 21, 2013,
http://www.dol.gov/opa/media/press/ilab/ILAB20131494.htm.   http://www.dol.gov/opa/media/press/ilab/ILAB20131494.htm

[34] SFRC staff discussion, Dhaka, August 2013.

[35] Della, Gloria. U.S. Department of Labor [News Release], "ILAB," July 29, 2013, accessed November 21, 2013,
http://www.dol.gov/opa/media/press/ilab/ILAB20131494.htm.http://www.dol.gov/opa/media/press/ilab/ILAB20131494.htm

[36] SFRC staff discussion, Washington, D.C. November 2013.

[37] SFRC staff discussion, Washington, D.C. November 2013.

[38] SFRC staff discussion, Dhaka, August 2013.

[39] SFRC staff discussion, Dhaka, August 2013.

[40] SFRC staff discussion, Dhaka, August 2013.

[41] SFRC staff discussion, Dhaka, August 2013.

[42] United States Agency for International Development. ''USG Programs to Improve Labor Conditions in Bangladesh.'' July 15, 2013.

[43] SFRC staff discussion, Washington, D.C. November 2013.

[44] SFRC staff discussion, Washington, D.C. November 2013.

[45] SFRC staff discussion, Washington, D.C. November 2013.

[46] ''Q&A on the Better Work Programme in Bangladesh.'' October 22, 2013. http://betterwork.org/global/?p=3712

[47] SFRC staff discussion, Washington, D.C. November 2013.

[48] SFRC staff discussion, Washington, D.C. November 2013.